END OF COURSE REVIEW

prepared for the course team by
kath woodward, david goldblatt and hugh mackay

This publication forms part of an Open University course DD100 *An Introduction to the Social Sciences: Understanding Social Change*. Details of this and other Open University courses can be obtained from the Course Information and Advice Centre, PO Box 724, The Open University, Milton Keynes MK7 6ZS, United Kingdom: tel. +44 (0)1908 653231, e-mail general-enquiries@open.ac.uk

Alternatively, you may visit the Open University website at http://www.open.ac.uk where you can learn more about the wide range of courses and packs offered at all levels by The Open University.

To purchase a selection of Open University course materials visit the webshop at www.ouw.co.uk, or contact Open University Worldwide, Michael Young Building, Walton Hall, Milton Keynes MK7 6AA, United Kingdom for a brochure. tel. +44 (0)1908 858785; fax +44 (0)1908 858787; e-mail ouwenq@open.ac.uk

The Open University
Walton Hall, Milton Keynes
MK7 6AA

First published 2000. Second edition 2001. Third edition 2004

Edited, designed and typeset by The Open University.

Printed and bound in the United Kingdom by the Alden Group, Oxford

ISBN 0 7492 5368 1

3.1

10242B/dd100endisbn074925368li3.1

Contents

The DD100 course team

John Allen, *Professor of Geography*

Penny Bennett, *Editor*

Pam Berry, *Compositor*

Simon Bromley, *Senior Lecturer in Government*

Lydia Chant, *Course Manager*

Stephen Clift, *Editor*

Allan Cochrane, *Professor of Public Policy*

Lene Connolly, *Print Buying Controller*

Jonathan Davies, *Graphic Designer*

Graham Dawson, *Lecturer in Economics*

Alison Edwards, *Editor*

Ross Fergusson, *Staff Tutor in Social Policy (Region 02)*

Fran Ford, *Senior Course Co-ordination Secretary*

Ian Fribbance, *Staff Tutor in Economics (Region 01)*

David Goldblatt, *Co-Course Team Chair*

Richard Golden, *Production and Presentation Administrator*

Jenny Gove, *Lecturer in Psychology*

Peter Hamilton, *Lecturer in Sociology*

Celia Hart, *Picture Researcher*

David Held, *Professor of Politics and Sociology*

Susan Himmelweit, *Professor of Economics*

Stephen Hinchliffe, *Lecturer in Geography*

Wendy Hollway, *Professor of Psychology*

Gordon Hughes, *Senior Lecturer in Social Policy*

Wendy Humphreys, *Staff Tutor in Government (Region 01)*

Jonathan Hunt, *Co-publishing Advisor*

Christina Janoszka, *Course Manager*

Pat Jess, *Staff Tutor in Geography (Region 12)*

Bob Kelly, *Staff Tutor in Government (Region 06)*

Margaret Kiloh, *Staff Tutor in Social Policy (Region 13)*

Sylvia Lay-Flurrie, *Secretary*

Gail Lewis, *Senior Lecturer in Social Policy*

Siân Lewis, *Graphic Designer*

Liz McFall, *Lecturer in Sociology*

Tony McGrew, *Professor of International Relations, University of Southampton*

Hugh Mackay, *Staff Tutor in Sociology (Region 10)*

Maureen Mackintosh, *Professor of Economics*

Eugene McLaughlin, *Senior Lecturer in Criminology and Social Policy*

Andrew Metcalf, *Senior Producer, BBC*

Gerry Mooney, *Staff Tutor in Social Policy (Region 11)*

Lesley Moore, *Senior Course Co-ordination Secretary*

Ray Munns, *Graphic Artist*

Karim Murji, *Senior Lecturer in Sociology*

Sarah Neal, *Lecturer in Social Policy*

Kathy Pain, *Staff Tutor in Geography (Region 02)*

Clive Pearson, *Tutor Panel*

Ann Phoenix, *Professor of Psychology*

Lynn Poole, *Tutor Panel*

Raia Prokhovnik, *Senior Lecturer in Government*

Norma Sherratt, *Staff Tutor in Sociology (Region 03)*

Roberto Simonetti, *Lecturer in Economics*

Dick Skellington, *Project Officer*

Brenda Smith, *Staff Tutor in Psychology (Region 12)*

Mark Smith, *Senior Lecturer in Government*

Matt Staples, *Course Manager*

Grahame Thompson, *Professor of Political Economy*

Ken Thompson, *Professor of Sociology*

Diane Watson, *Staff Tutor in Sociology (Region 05)*

Stuart Watt, *Lecturer in Psychology*

Andy Whitehead, *Graphic Artist*

Kath Woodward, *Course Team Chair, Senior Lecturer in Sociology*

Chris Wooldridge, *Editor*

External Assessor

Nigel Thrift, *Professor of Geography, University of Oxford*

1 INTRODUCTION

1.1 Block overview

Almost there! Your work on Block 6 and the final TMA, TMA 06, will occupy the last three weeks of your study time on DD100 and then you will have finished. As usual, the course materials and recommended route through them are detailed below in Figures 1 and 2. Block 6, the *End of Course Review* is, as its title suggests, organized around reviewing the course. This is

Study week	Course material	Suggested study time
31	*End of Course Review* Audio-cassette 10, Sides A and B	36 hours
32 and 33	TMA 06	

FIGURE 1   Course materials for Block 6

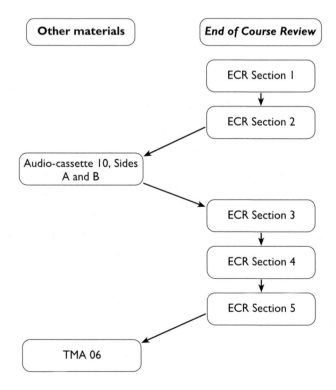

FIGURE 2
Recommended study route for Block 6

also very important at this stage in DD100 because you need to do this in order to prepare for TMA 06, which requires you to select material from across the whole of DD100. The block is structured around the course themes and, in particular, a major concern of DD100, change in UK society, especially from the period following the Second World War to the present. In order to help you recap some of the key issues addressed in DD100 and to think back over what have been both key areas of change and key debates within the social sciences, Block 6 uses the trigger of the changing features of the city.

1.2   Aims of the block

The main purpose of Block 6 is to give you an opportunity to synthesize and integrate materials across the whole of DD100. This is what you need to be able to do in order to answer TMA 06, so the *End of Course Review* is organized around giving you plenty of practice at making links and connections between different parts of the course and between different ideas within the social sciences. The key skills that drive your work on Block 6 are those that you started developing in Block 5: selection of material, synthesis and integration. TMA 05 asked you to draw on material from different parts of the block but TMA 06 asks you to range across the whole course, not just one block, in bringing together material from different blocks into a coherent essay. In addition, you will find yourself drawing on a whole range of other skills in Block 6 that you have developed through the course, such as reading visual images, maps and evidence and weighing up which material is most relevant.

Our starting point is some questions about the city. The contemporary city could be seen as a microcosm of the changes that have taken place in recent years and as particularly appropriate illustration of DD100's concern with understanding social change. We are going to use some images and texts which evoke different aspects of cities in order to trigger a review of the course and to help you to think about some strategies which you can use in TMA 06.

1.3   Assessing Block 6

As with the rest of DD100 your work on Block 6 is all part of what you need to do for an assignment. In this case it is TMA 06. As with TMA 04 and TMA 05, we will be asking you to write a 1,500 word essay. However, this time you will need to draw on material from at least three blocks of DD100. It will be important to decide how to select relevant material and then to integrate ideas and evidence from these different parts of the course into a well-organized essay. More detail on what to do will be in the student notes for TMA 06. Audio-cassette 10, Side A, which is a discussion between course team members, also provides guidance on the skills needed to tackle this assignment.

2 CITY THEMES

The purpose of this section is to:

- Use the topic of the city to review some of the social changes which have been identified in DD100.

- Develop skills of reflecting on materials which you have already studied.

- Develop skills of selecting appropriate material, synthesizing and integrating by exploring connections between the ideas about the city which are represented here and your own notes on earlier blocks of DD100.

Before you go on, you may want to look back to some earlier parts of the course where these skills have been discussed and some key techniques have been explored. For example:

Introductory Workbook, Section 7 on reflection.

Workbook 3, the summary in Section 6 on revision skills.

You will also need your own notes and summaries from the earlier blocks to hand as you work through the following material.

2.1 The city

Why have we picked the city as a trigger topic? The city is a significant site of change. City life can be seen in popular imaginings as fast moving, often in contrast to the apparently slower pace of life in the country. Cities are places where many people live, with the vast majority of the population in the UK living in the conurbations rather than the countryside. Although the population of London declined slightly at the start of the twenty-first century it still has a population of 7 million out of a UK population of 59.9 million (*Social Trends*, 2003). The sheer size of cities, with some cities worldwide having populations of 20 million, and the scale of their institutions and infrastructure make the city a key focus for social change.

What associations does the idea of the city conjure up for you? Maybe you think about the city in which you live. Maybe you think of a particular city or perhaps of what makes the city different from the countryside, with the city representing a hectic pace and change in contrast to the apparent tradition and stability of the countryside. This opposition between the city and the countryside, the urban and the rural is an on-going theme, and part of the sometimes unstated but ever-present meaning that is attached to cities.

FIGURE 3 City life: on the move? Traffic gridlock

FIGURE 4 The rural idyll: Constable's *The Haywain*

The city is often contrasted with the rural idyll that is associated
mythologically with rural life. In the UK the notion of the rolling, especially
English countryside is often invoked as part of the true British, certainly
English identity. Images such as thatched cottages, cricket played on village
greens, and the music of Edward Elgar all connote, albeit idealized and
probably quite unrealistic but nonetheless very influential, ideas about an

English or British identity which counters the rural with the urban within the context of a 'natural' reading of the rural in relation to a social construction of the city made by human beings. Such rural imaginings may also be predominantly white and seen to represent much less diverse and varied culture and ethnicity than the multi-ethnic city. Think back to Block 1 where we looked at examples of national identity such as Englishness (Book 1, Chapter 4) or the television programme, *Defining Moments*, where we looked at historically changing notions of being British.

The idealization of the countryside has as its counterpart the ravages of nineteenth century industrialization as described by Friedrich Engels, who commented on the conditions under which factory workers lived in Manchester in 1845:

> nothing but narrow, filthy nooks and alleys ... Everywhere half or wholly ruined buildings, some of them actually uninhabited, which means a great deal here; rarely a wooden or stone floor to be seen in the houses, almost uniformly broken, ill-fitting windows and doors, and a state of filth! ...

> Enough! The whole side of the Irk [the river] is built in this way, a planless, knotted chaos of houses, more or less on the verge of uninhabitableness, whose unclean interiors fully correspond with their filthy external surroundings.

> (Engels, 1987, first published 1845, p.91)

Another, somewhat different story of the city sees city life as modern and exciting in contrast to the out-dated tradition of rural life. However, both versions contrast the two, and locate our understanding of the city in relation to the countryside.

The two sides of this opposition between city and countryside are differently valued. Whilst the countryside may be seen to represent peace and stability and some degree of affluence in popular culture, city life may also be marked by poverty and inequality and city streets may be seen as thronging with criminals, as part of a moral panic as suggested in the *Introductory Chapter*. Rural poverty and rural crime are frequently overlooked in the construction of the rural idyll, as was argued in Chapter 4 of Block 1 and on Audio-cassette 5, Side A.

These popular imaginings about the city and the different stories which inform everyday thinking are, of course, contradictory. On the one hand, the city is exciting and dynamic and full of new opportunities and, on the other, it is a hotbed of criminality and a site of poverty and inequality. The countryside is represented as idyllic, ignoring the reality of poverty, lack of resources, jobs and services experienced by many, though certainly not all, who live there.

Not only are there divisions between the city and the countryside, there are divisions within cities. For example, cities may be divided along class, cultural, religious or ethnic lines. In 1991, the English writer Tony Parker went to Belfast. He stayed for over a year compiling a book of interviews with a wide range of the city's people. When trying to find a local assistant, whom he hoped might be personable, reliable, capable of keeping confidences and so on, the conversation soon turned to the issue of names.

> Of one, the first thing I'd been told was 'she'd be ideal, because her name's Teresa Green. So with a Catholic Christian name and a good sound Protestant surname, she could use either – which'd be a terrific advantage.' Someone recommending someone else said: 'She'd be most suitable: her name's Barbara you see, which is completely non-informative. In fact she's a Protestant but she's married to a Catholic – though she only says so when it's necessary. Another thing is they live in Stranmillis, which nowadays everybody knows of as a mixed Bohemian area, so that'd be a plus too.' Part of the description of a third person was: 'Her only drawback is she spent some of her childhood in Cheltenham, so she sometimes comes out with an English accent now and again without realising it.'
>
> (Parker, 1994, pp.2–3)

Reflecting on the experience Parker wrote: 'these introductory remarks about Christian and surnames, where people lived and what sort of accent they had, were all offering me an important glimpse, if only I'd been able to see it, of the totally different world I was to inhabit and become immersed in' (Parker, 1994, p.3). The Belfast of 1991 that Parker immersed himself in was a city where identity and place, nation and culture, were defining features of everyday life. Despite the progress of the peace process since Parker left Belfast, identity and its relationship to place (different parts of Belfast), to nation (Ireland and the UK), to religious tradition (Catholic or Protestant), and to politics (Nationalist and Unionist) still defines who you are and where you think you come from. The city of Belfast has clearly differentiated areas associated with Catholics and others with Protestants (Figure 5).

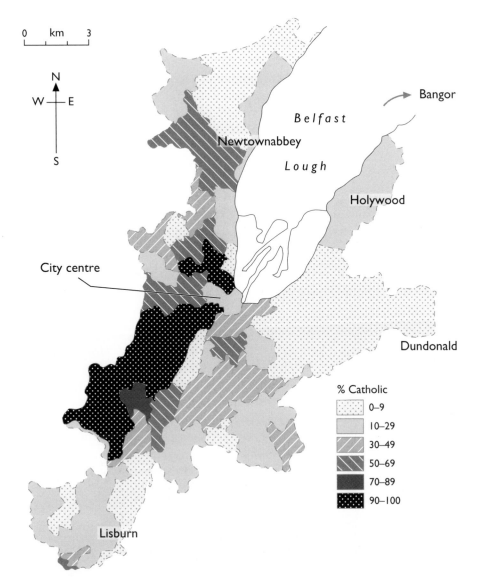

FIGURE 5   Distribution of Catholic population in Belfast, 1991
Source: Boal, 1995, p29

Although there is a high concentration of population within a relatively limited geographical space, there is still divided space within cities. The occupation of different space within cities has changed, for example different immigrant groups have come to stay in particular areas of cities, such as Jewish people in the early 1900s in the East End of London followed by Bangladeshis following the Second World War in the same area of the city. The occupation of space within cities has changed but these divisions have traditionally been linked to factors such as class, ethnicity and culture. To take Cardiff, the capital city of Wales, as an example, there is a history of the occupation of inner and outer city areas along class lines.

> Coalowners lived outside Cardiff, their investments were in the coalfield and in
> coaling stations throughout the world ... The 'legitimate' middlemen in coal had
> worldwide investments and were often part of national rather purely local concerns
> ... The shipowners were similarly distant from the local society ... these men were in
> but not of Cardiff, they had an office there but no real economic interest. It would
> not particularly have harmed these men if Cardiff did become a 'ruin as literally and
> lamentably as Carthage of old'. To them Cardiff docks were indeed no more than 'a
> convenience and economical means of carrying on their business'.

(Daunton, 1977, p.155)

Another area of division was between different areas within the city with dockland areas of ports being associated with particular groups. In Cardiff the dockland area is known as Butetown.

Glenn Jordan, a North American anthropologist who studies Butetown, has listed the following as represented in Butetown in the past 150 years:

> Irish, Welsh, English, Scots, Turks, Cypriots, French, French-speaking West Indians
> (presumably from Martinique and/or Guadeloupe), Jamaicans, Barbadians,
> Trinidadians, Guyanese, British Hondurans, Panamanians, Bahamians, St Lucians,
> St Kittsians, Germans, Spanish, Portuguese, Cape Verdeans, Maltese, Italians,
> Chinese, Japanese, Malays, Indians (that is, people from what is now Pakistan,
> India and Bangladesh), Somalis, Yemeni, Egyptians, Jews, Poles, Estonians,
> Latvians, Ukrainians, Norwegians, Finns, Danes, Mauritians, Sierra Leoneans,
> Liberians, Nigerians, Cameroonians, Gambians, Ghanaians, Angolans, South
> Africans, North Americans and a few others (for example, one Maori and at
> least one Fijian). ... Nearly all of the immigrants to Cardiff docklands were male –
> and virtually all of them settled in the Butetown area. Once there, they met and
> often married women from the South Wales valleys and other parts of the British
> Isles. Today, most of Butetown's residents (and former residents) are of 'mixed'
> ethnic heritage. It is very common to find families from the area that are Muslim and
> Christian and Black and White: indeed such families are far more common than
> ones that are only one race or only one religion. One well-known family is of West
> Indian, West European and Chinese origin; the origins of another are Somali (Sunni
> Muslim) and Russian Jewish. Nobody who is from Butetown finds this 'odd': it is
> only outsiders who do. ... This is a genuinely cosmopolitan community, inordinately
> rich in culture – and, crucially, in cross-cultural and inter-racial understanding.

(Jordan and Weedon, 1995, pp.135–6)

This extract challenges the notion that ethnic diversity is a very new feature of UK cities, at least in this particular case. Cities are characterized by different patterns of spatial organization and different social divisions. The mobility and migration of peoples in the late twentieth and early twenty-first centuries has led to an expansion of the diversity of life in cities, especially in the West.

Different occupation of space also arises from the redevelopment of areas within cities. For example, the development of the derelict Cardiff docklands in the late 1980s led to its promotion as a 'vibrant' space for the pursuit of leisure.

FIGURE 6   Magazine advertisement for Cardiff Bay, May 1992

In introducing the topic of the city, we can see that our discussion has already drawn on some key issues in DD100, both in terms of the course themes and some of the big issues in the course.

- Cities are linked to change and present the location and focus of many important and far-reaching social changes
- The city is contrasted with the countryside in a version of the distinction between the natural and the social, with the rural being associated with what is 'natural' and the city as social, cultural and produced through human agency
- Cities are the subject of myths and stories, including moral panics
- Cities are associated with poverty and inequality as well as new opportunities and diversity
- Cities are spatially organized and the occupancy of these spaces is linked to social divisions
- The city is the focus of social, economic, cultural and political divisions which pervade contemporary social relations.

In order to move this discussion along we are going to look in a bit more detail at how your study of DD100 could inform your view of the city, by considering some images of contemporary city life.

ACTIVITY 1

Look at these five photographs of contemporary city life. What features would you pick out, which are explored in DD100, as aspects of change in UK society?

FIGURE 7   Street scene: cultural diversity?

FIGURE 8   Greater availability of products?

FIGURE 9   Looking for somewhere to live

FIGURE 10   British Museum: glass dome

COMMENT

Each of these images presents different aspects of contemporary city life that are taken up in DD100.

The first image (Figure 7) represents one dimension of diversity in the city and the multiplicity of cultures which are included in just one aspect of contemporary life. The 'global city' illustrates the globalization of economies and culture that are explored in Book 4, *A Globalizing World?* in Chapters 2 and 3. The inclusion of a diverse range of products and patterns of consumption examples of Book 5, Chapter 4's discussion of the consumer society, illustrated in Figures 7 and 8, may not in themselves signify a great deal of choice for everyone, but they are indicative of the diversity of city life in a globalized culture and of the wide range of identities that might be available in the city. This image represents particularly positive aspects of the global city in the multi-ethnicity that characterizes urban life.

FIGURE 11 Heathrow: moving between cities

Figure 9 suggests that whilst Figure 8 may indicate that the contemporary Western city might be characterized by a greater availability of products and more diverse patterns of consumption than at any time in history, there is also inequality and poverty and these goods and services are not available to everyone. International companies have a high street presence in major cities across the world, but for those without the resources to purchase their goods, there is very little choice. Class-based identities still shape patterns of consumption as was argued in Book 1, *Questioning Identity*, Chapter 3. Major cities are the location of excitement, opportunities and the exercise of agency manifest in cultural diversity and the abundance of consumer products, but they are also the site of poverty, homelessness, uncertainty and instability.

Figure 10 is a familiar representation of the city as home to new architectural designs. This one includes a change of use with the dome and well lit space of the redesigned courtyard at the British Museum. This image raises different issues, firstly that of space. Cities offer a concentration of population and of resources. Limited space and high population demand radical, imaginative, technologically innovative solutions in housing, the workplace and leisure spaces. The second issue highlighted here is that of technology and the advances of the 'knowledge society'. Cities are the focus of the knowledge revolution, the source and practice of technological innovation with economies based on ICT and the new technologies.

The last picture (Figure 11) also highlights the impact of technological advance and most strikingly the development of networks between cities worldwide. Cities deal in movement across continents and in mobile populations, sucking in workers from rural areas through migration and immigration and are core to the understanding of globalization. Cities are the nodes for networks and flows of people and of knowledge. The speed of connection between cities is illustrated here in relation to the physical movement of people, although other networks of communication, for example based on the Internet, offer even faster networks, a point which is important, especially at a time of ever slower moving traffic in city centres and, in the UK in particular, heavy delays on trains and other forms of public transport.

How have we drawn on DD100 in our comments here? Which concepts or theories have we used? One key issue is that of the idea of globalization, which is well illustrated in these images in many different aspects. Another is the notion of identity, especially in relation to place. We have also drawn on some of the key aspects of change that are identified in DD100: changing knowledge, the advent of the 'consumer' as well as the 'knowledge society', changing occupation of space, movement of people and of knowledge, changing articulations between the natural and the social, and the changing role of social, cultural and political institutions. We have also drawn on the course themes, for example in considering the extent to which people in cities are increasingly able to exercise agency and how far they may be increasingly constrained by social structures. The city may offer diversity, but it is also a site of uncertainty. Cities can be seen as central to the development of new knowledges and the transmission of new ideas.

Now is a good moment to stop your reading of the *End of Course Review* and listen to Audio-cassette 10.

Side A offers some discussion which will guide your work on TMA 06, which is the key focus of this block. It will give you practical advice on preparing and writing TMA 06. Side B has a discussion about cities and change, which covers some of the ground we have included in Sections 1 and 2 above. The discussion between Ken Worpole, Doreen Massey and David Goldblatt is very useful for addressing questions about social change which feature in the options for TMA 06. Audio-cassette 10 is important material for TMA 06.

 Now please listen to Audio-cassette 10, Side A and Side B and read the accompanying notes and then return to this point in the *End of Course Review*.

3 LOOKING BACK OVER THE COURSE

In this section we would like you to think back over the course, using your own notes and summarizing some of the material from the work you have already done which should provide a useful resource when you come to write TMA 06.

ACTIVITY 2

Look back over your notes on Block 1. If you have not collected them or reduced them, take the opportunity now to have a go.

You may want to work with the questions and techniques we suggest below.

However you go about doing this, please, please do it yourself first. Our attempt at the notes below is for discussion and comparison. They're not definitive or comprehensive, nor do they necessarily reflect your understanding of the course. *We cannot emphasize enough that you will only prepare yourself properly for TMA 06 by doing your own notes.*

Questions

- What were the key questions of the block?
- In what way were the course themes used? What kinds of questions did they raise?
- In what ways did each chapter in the block address these issues? What were the key debates in each chapter? What different or opposing perspectives were used to explore the materials?
- What were the key case studies, the best examples and the types of empirical evidence used?
- What additional ideas from the audio-cassettes, TV programme and associated supplement can you use?

Techniques

- Skim your own notes and/or the Introductions and Afterwords to the main textbooks.
- Skim the introductory sections to the workbooks, your own notes and efforts on key summarizing activities in the workbooks (grids, tables, diagrammatic notes), and any work you did in connection with the consolidation and reflection section of each workbook.
- Skim and note the summaries of each chapter. Better still, use your own notes for this.

C O M M E N T

Our quick notes looked like this:

QUESTIONS

1 How identities formed?

2 Extent we can shape identities?

3 Uncertainty about identity?

THEMES

U+D

Are identities more complex, diverse; decline in stereotypes, emergence of new and multiple identities? Challenges to racialized catgeories?

Uncertainties around Britishness, Englishness, masculinity, old models of class society?

S+A

Explores relative weight S+A in identity formation. Different structures – social, biological, cultural, political and economic.

Recognizes individual agency, collective agency resistance, e.g. countering racism, new social movements.

K+K

Question-driven social science.

Introduction to circuit of knowledge in workbook, Sect. 1.4.

Role of evidence, categories, e.g. Census, which produce meanings.

CHAPTERS AND DEBATES

Ch. 1

Concept of identity.

Mead, Goffman and Freud.

Althusser and social structures.

Ch. 2

Sex and gender.

Role biological, social structures.

Problem of fuzzy categories.

Theory self-categorization.

Impact of gender identities on school performance – Murphy and Elwood.

Ch. 3

Understands economic structures in terms of poverty, income, work and wealth.

Marx vs. Weber models of stratification.

Work vs. consumption as source of identity.

Social polarization vs. social fragmentation.

Ch. 4

Relationship: identity, 'race', 'ethnicity', gender and place.

Cultural representations e.g. media of ethnicized identities.

Ethnicized identities shaped by cultural, geographical, economic and political structures, and conscious agency.

Explanations of ethnicization and racialization.

EVIDENCE AND EXAMPLES

Ch. 1

Sarup; passport.

Greaves – autobiographical writing.

Kay – poem.

Ch. 2

Bem's Sex Role Inventory test.

Conversational and observational analysis of children.

Statistical data on exam performance.

Observation of classroom practice.

Ch. 3

Statistical evidence on wealth, poverty, income.

Interviews with people on low income.

Case study of call centres.

Ch. 4

Interview material on ethnicized and racialized identities.

Census categories.

Englishness as case study, analysis of texts, e.g. media reports.

AUDIO AND TV

See esp. TV 01 – Diana vs. Churchill, contrast in representation and sense of Britishness, decline of old elites, new populism and diversity, role of mass media.

How did your notes compare with ours?

Let us emphasize again: *you do not need to be producing comprehensive notes or notes identical to ours.*

What you should be producing is a set of notes that you can use to help you prepare for TMA 06, which will require you to draw on material from at least three blocks of DD100. You may find it useful to have a look at the TMA booklet now. It will be clearer what kinds of materials connected to what issues you will need to be looking out for.

You may find that you have too many notes or that our suggestions for organizing the material are unhelpful or that the whole process is proving rather fraught. If so:

1   Take a look at Box 1 below which lays out one model of generating condensed notes from course materials.

2   Call your tutor or other students you are in contact with to discuss it.

3   Have another go at taking shorter, sharper notes from your first notes.

BOX 1	**Condensing your notes**

Is it worth writing new notes at this stage in the course?

Yes, it is an excellent idea to work with a pen in your hand, actually creating something as you work! This gives a much more constructive feel to the tasks of revision and synthesis and will engage your mind more effectively for long spells of work. One very good way of working is as follows:

> Make *very condensed* notes from various books, notes, etc. that you have gathered together for revision on a particular *topic*.
>
> Then extract the main points from these condensed notes to produce a single *summary sheet* of headings with key points, names, etc. for that *topic*.
>
> Finally, having done this for the topics within a given section of the course, take the main headings from all the topic summary sheets and produce a single *main summary sheet* which outlines the main subject matter for that whole *section* of the course.

The effort to 'boil' the course down in this way, so as to extract its concentrated essence, is extremely valuable because it converts the broad themes and the detailed discussions of the course into a form which is much more manageable for the purposes of writing TMA 06 and, on future courses, for answering questions in exams.

What is more, when you come to answering TMA 06, you can remind yourself from the *main summary sheet*, to identify what main topics lie within the section. You then work out which of the topics are relevant to the question and remind yourself of the *topic summary sheets* concerned. You scan mentally through the main items on any given topic summary sheet and select whichever are relevant. This then leads you back towards the condensed notes which 'lie behind' those items on the topic summary sheet. In other words, having, in your revision, constructed pathways *down* from the basic source materials through condensed notes and topic summary sheets to a master summary sheet, you can then quickly trace your way back *up* those pathways, to locate exactly the material that is relevant to the question. Perhaps the practice is rarely quite as neat as that, but at least this 'note-condensing' approach gives you the basis for a systematic over-viewing and retrieval system.

Furthermore, a strategy such as this gives you a well-focused and absorbing task to be getting on with, rather than the aimless scanning back over old material which sends you to sleep and dulls your spirits. Finally, condensed notes will supply you with just the kind of 'pulled together' version of the course which will be invaluable in the future, when you want to remind yourself of what the course was about.

Next, we would like you to use the material on cities with which we started this block to consider links between the city as a trigger topic and the work you have done on each of the blocks of DD100. This will give you some practice in synthesizing material from different parts of the course and in making connections between different ideas in the social sciences. To start off we would like you to try to link what we have been thinking about in relation to the city and social change with your notes from Block 1.

ACTIVITY 3

What links can you draw between the material on cities in Section 2 and Block 1?

COMMENT

We came up with this summary on the city and identity:

- Cities are a source of both collective and individual identities.
- Cities are characterized by uniformity and diversity, proximity and distance, inclusion and exclusion.
- City identities combine with, and shape, other identities: 'ethnicity', class and gender.
- Cities can be places of uncertainty and uncertain identities, and of new, diverse opportunities.
- Cities can be thought of as a complex amalgamation of structures: social, economic, cultural, physical. These structures both shape identities and provide the context for, and possibility of, conscious active agency and choice in identity formation.

ACTIVITY 4

Look back over your notes on Block 2. If you have not collected them or reduced them, take the opportunity now to have a go. We are going to work with the same set of questions as we did in Activity 2.

- What were the key questions of the block?
- In what way were the course themes used?
- In what ways did each chapter in the block address these issues? What were the key debates in each chapter?
- What were the key case studies, the best examples and the types of empirical evidence used?
- What additional ideas from the audio-cassette, TV programme and associated supplement can you use?

COMMENT

Our quick notes looked like this:

QUESTIONS

1 How can we best think about the intermixing of the natural and the social?

2 Impact of mixed views of the soc. and nat. in context of environmental uncertainties and risks?

3 How can soc. sci. help us think about 1 and 2?

THEMES

U+D

Diversity of ways of knowing, describing thinking about the soc./ nat. - reflected in different and diverse accounts of human nature, different models of health, origins of disasters.

Uncertainty - rising levels of environmental danger and risk, conflicts over interpretation of risk, possibility of risk society?

S+A

Complex interaction of natural/biological structures (bodies and environments) with social structures (models of explanation, social interests, etc.) all help structure human behaviour and beliefs. Model of markets strong on relationship by S+A, esp. recreation of S by outcomes of A.

K+K

Historical developments - changing and diverse knowledge of human nature, health, environmental risks.

Explanations – use of evidence, interpretation of evidence, variable methods in soc. sci.

Contrasts with natural sciences.

CHAPTERS AND DEBATES

Ch. 1

Different approaches to human nature. Distinction between humans and other animals: symbolization, consciousness. Different balance of S+A, natural and social, conception of what is meant by nat. and soc.

Ch. 2

Four models of health and illness, all different conceptions and weight given to soc. and nat. structures, types of evidence, models of practice (medical science vs. social model vs. complementary med. vs. New Public Health).

Ch. 3

Model of market neo-classical – to explain environmental degradation. Critiques of model – ignorance of externalities, public goods, problems, etc.

Ch. 4

Conflicting models of explaining natural disasters – natural science vs. social science. Conflicting models of interpreting BSE, uncertainties in public reception of science, emergence of a risk society?

EVIDENCE AND EXAMPLES

Ch. 1

Wide range of evidence used by different approaches to human nature, social, psychological, scientific interpretations.

Ch. 2

Different evidence for different models of health. Scientific method for medical science. Quantitative data on class and mortality for social model. Qualitative personal reporting for complementary methods. Risk analysis for New PH.

Ch. 3

Exhaustible resources, common resources and pubic goods, externalities.

Ch. 4

Flooding in England. Hurricane Mitch. BSE.

<u>AUDIO AND TV</u>

TV 02 – strong on diversity of interpretations of relationship between natural and social – viewed through the example of disability. Challenge to dominant models reflects some of health debate. Good example of the value of qualitative evidence, personal narratives.

Now that you have sorted out your notes on Block 2, let's try out the same exercise of making links between Block 2 and our earlier discussion of cities.

ACTIVITY 5

How can you apply your notes on Block 2 to the discussion of the city in Section 2?

COMMENT

We came up with this summary on the city and the natural and the social:

- The city should be thought about as a complex interaction of natural and social systems, although it is often thought of as diametrically opposed to a pure natural countryside.

- Cities are major sites of environmental problems both within the city and elsewhere.

- Environmental and social problems are closely intertwined.

- Some cities are more environmentally problematic than others.

ACTIVITY 6

Look back over your notes on Block 3. If you have not collected them or reduced them, take the opportunity now to have a go. We are going to work with the same set of questions as we did in Activity 2.

- What were the key questions of the block?

- In what way were the course themes used?

- In what ways did each chapter in the block address these issues? What were the key debates in each chapter?

- What were the key case studies, the best examples and the types of empirical evidence used?

- What additional ideas from the audio-cassette and TV programme can you use?

C O M M E N T

Our quick notes looked like this:

QUESTIONS

1 How do social institutions order lives?

2 How does power work in and through social institutions to order lives?

3 How have political ideologies influenced changes in power and ordering?

THEMES

U+D

Are changes in social institutions and their ordering producing uncertainty? Are the characteristics of family life, working life and the welfare sate creating uncertainty? Why?

Is there an increasing diversity to the institutions of work, welfare and the family?

Is this a source of uncertainty? Is it a source of liberation, increasing choice? For whom?

S+A

Social institutions operate as structures both constraining agency and providing opportunities for agency.

The structure of institutions helps determine who is empowered and who is constrained by those structures.

Key link – all structures create and distribute power – in its many forms.

K+K

What knowledge counts? Changing knowledge over time. Shifting fortunes and strengths of political ideologies have helped initiate, support and legitimize structural changes in family life, work and welfare provision. Knowledge in general and political ideologies in particular is a source of social power.

How do we know? Status of evidence. Explores how claims and concepts combine to generate theories that can do explanatory work. Looks at how theories are shaped by the moral/normative values they embrace and how theories shape what kinds of evidence one draws on and how that evidence is interpreted.

CHAPTERS AND DEBATES

Ch. 1

Develops vocabulary for describing power – persuasion, coercion, domination, etc.

Offers two models of theorizing power – Weber and Foucault, power from above and below.

Offers explanations of expert authority and power (see Block 5 on experts).

Tests theories of power in connection with call centre.

Ch. 2

Account of family change – explores character of diversity and link to uncertainty.

Contrasts feminist and conservative accounts of change and its consequences.

Note different moral perspectives of these ideologies shape theoretical argument.

Ch. 3

Account of shift in labour market from security to insecurity, inflexibility to flexibility.

Compares liberal and social democratic accounts of labour markets and connection to macroeconomic issues.

Ch. 4

Account of shift in welfare state from 'golden age' of security to insecurity – but contrast exaggerated.

EVIDENCE AND EXAMPLES

Ch. 1

GM foods debate on modes of power, role of experts. Call centres to explore Weber vs. Foucault and use of theory.

Ch. 2

Quantitative data on shifting structure of family life.

Ch. 3

Quantitative data on flexibility in labour market gender differences.

Case studies of Rover to illuminate role of power in changing labour market.

Ch. 4

Transformation of welfare state under Conservatives, 1979-97, as case study for exploring restructuring of institutions, role of social values and ideologies in shaping change. Critique of New Labour developments in context of social change.

AUDIO AND TV

TV 03 – qualitative evidence through diversity of personal biographies of generational shift in attitude to security, identity and work. Anecdotal evidence of diversity of change in the labour market and the structural creation of both insecurity and opportunity.

AC 5 – historical evidence and analysis of recent developments and references to quantitative and qualitative evidence and critiques of change. Use of theory.

Now that you have put together your notes on Block 3 let's move on to doing the same kind of exercise that we did for Blocks 1 and 2 and try making some links between Block 3 and the city.

ACTIVITY 7

How might you apply this material from Block 3 to our discussion of the city?

COMMENT

We came up with this summary on the city and order and power:

- Cities are sites of both social order and disorder, linked to and shaping other patterns and institutions of social order, e.g. families/work.
- Cities' diversity and messiness can tend towards social disorder.
- The organization of cities is often a top-down approach to power and policy, which does not empower the majority of people who live in the city.
- There are enormous differences in power between different urban actors, communities, groups who are divided by class, ethnicity and gender.

ACTIVITY 8

Look back over your notes on Block 4. If you have not collected them or reduced them, take the opportunity now to have a go. We are going to work with the same set of questions as we did in Activity 2.

- What were the key questions of the block?

- In what way were the course themes used?

- In what ways did each chapter in the block address these issues? What were the key debates in each chapter?

- What were the key case studies, the best examples and the types of empirical evidence used?

- What additional ideas from the audio-cassettes, TV programme and associated supplement can you use?

C O M M E N T

Our quick notes looked like this:

QUESTIONS

1 What is meant by globalization? How best conceived?

2 Are claims about contemporary globalization significant? Historical comparisons?

3 If globalization is significant what is its impact on autonomy and sovereignty of nation-state?

4 Winners and losers?

THEMES

U+D

Uncertainty – old order of sovereign nation-sates and Westphalia international order undermined by globalization – uncertainty about role, power and legitimacy of nation-states, international organizations. Maybe more continuity and resistance to globalization. Not a new phenomenon or one of any great significance.

Diversity – cultural globalization force for national diversity – can also be seen as diminishing diversity through Americanization cultural imperialism, gendered, ethnicized inequalities.

S+A

Globalization creates new global structures (political, cultural, economic) which shape/constrain agency of individuals, nation-sates, people living in poverty, especially women, migrant people.

All structures have spatial dimension – global, regional, national, local.

Globalization produces new forms of agency – international NGOs and alliances, international organizations.

K+K

Cultural globalization force for spreading diversity of information to many, can undermine elite and expert knowledge.

Support for different claims. Introduces skill of evaluating strengths and weaknesses of theories and claims – through criteria of coherence, empirical adequacy, comprehensiveness.

CHAPTERS AND DEBATES

Ch. 1

Strong on models of globalization and vocabulary/ conceptualization for describing global networks – globalists vs. inter-nationalists vs. transformationalists.

Ch. 2

Highlights globalists' position. Presents globalists, inter-nationalists and transformationalists on impact of cultural globalization.

Notes interconnection of these positions with political ideologies (esp. in Workbook 4).

Ch. 3

Challenges dominance of globalization as new phenomenon. Presents inter-nationalist case on economic globalization. Explores origins of winners and losers economically. Reviews different perspectives on economic globalization, including feminist critiques and role of inequalities.

Ch. 4

Strong transformationalist position on cultural globalization. Explores some globalist and inter-nationalist critiques, esp. in Workbook 4. Contrasts contemporary international order with old Westphalia system. Explores origins of uncertainty. Possibility of re-regulating globalization.

EVIDENCE AND EXAMPLES

Ch. 1

Sets up debates, e.g. globalist/non-globalist positions. Draws up models of globalization through interconnectedness, infrastructure, etc. and explores types of evidence that would build on this.

Mapping globalization.

Good case study of environmental globalization.

Ch. 2

Strong use of quantitative data on TV exports and viewing.
Qualitative evidence on how TV is received and read by viewers.
Case study of telegraph vs. the Internet.

Ch. 3

Use of quantitative data to explore contemporary globalization and make historical comparisons. Offers evaluation of different evidence and argument about economic globalization. Review of different theoretical perspectives.

Ch. 4

Case studies main form of evidence – esp. MAI protest, regulating the drug trade. The East Asian financial crisis.

AUDIO AND TV

Audio – Giddens' lecture and conversation (AC 7, Sides A and B) good example of globalist/inter-nationalist arguments. AC 8, Side A discussion of globalization.

TV 04 – enriches the account of cultural globalization, interesting material on technological determinism, Japan case study good contrasts with UK focus of the book.

Now that you have put together another set of notes we want to try out your ideas on globalization in relation to the city.

ACTIVITY 9

How might you apply your notes on Block 4 to our discussion of the city?

COMMENT _____

We came up with this summary on the city and globalization:

- The impact of globalization on cities is diverse, acting through economic, environmental, political, cultural and migratory structures. There are winners and losers between cities and within cities.
- Cities are part of global communication networks.
- Cities are dynamic and changing, offering new opportunities as well as insecurity and uncertainties.
- Patterns of inequality persist, suggesting that globalization is not such a new phenomenon.

- Some global cities, such as London, have prospered economically at the price of intensified social polarization and disorder. Other cities, especially older manufacturing centres, have been negatively affected, especially when disconnected from global financial and service networks.

- Cities, as agents and containers of local structures, have responded in different localized ways.

ACTIVITY 10

The last block! Look back over your notes on Block 5. If you have not collected them or reduced them, take the opportunity now to have a go. We are going to work with the same set of questions as we did in Activity 2.

- What were the key questions of the block?

- In what way were the course themes used?

- In what ways did each chapter in the block address these issues? What were the key debates in each chapter?

- What were the key case studies, the best examples and the types of empirical evidence used?

- What additional ideas from the audio-cassette and TV programme can you use?

COMMENT _____

Our notes looked like this:

QUESTIONS

1   What is knowledge?

2   How is knowledge socially constructed?

3   Decline in trust of expert/elite knowledge?

4   Knowledge as a force of social change?

THEMES

U+D

Uncertainty and diversity very closely linked. Internal diversity of knowledge systems explored. Flowering of many competing knowledge systems in the same field explored. Both result in uncertainty amongst experts and this is communicated to the general public.

'Knowledge society', strong argument about diversity and uncertainty; 'risk society', similarly strong on uncertainty and conflict of interpretations centre stage.

S+A

Knowledge systems can act as structures, shaping agency – what we can and can't say/do/know. But also provide context for innovation, criticism, new forms of knowledge.

K+K

Explores origins and consequences of increasingly diverse/uncreated knowledge systems. Impact of new knowledges and ways of seeing world on wider social structures.

Places circuit of knowledge and social science knowledge in a social context.

Contrast different systems of knowledge and knowing by method, evidence, etc., natural science, social science, common sense, religion, etc., Ch. 1 and Ch. 2.

Contrast different social science methods – positivism vs. interpretative social science in Ch. 2.

Returns to role of moral/normative political argument, esp. Ch. 3.

Returns to problems of weighing up the arguments, Ch. 4.

CHAPTERS AND DEBATES

Ch. 1

Explores knowledge of health and illness as example of general issues in social construction of knowledge.

Explores four models of sociology of knowledge: Popper, Kuhn, Foucault and Fox Keller.

Explores role of language, power, institutions and social change in constructing and validating knowledge.

Ch. 2

Explores social construction of religious knowledge, Weber vs. Durkheim, substantive vs. functional models of religion.

Contrasts positivist and interpretative social science as model of explanation and investigation.

Focuses on secularization debate, rise of new spirituality, role of ethnicity and gender

Ch. 3

Explores diversity and uncertainly in realm of political ideologies.

Uses challenge of environmental problems and green arguments to highlight weakness and uncertainty amongst modern political ideological and political elites – example of declining trust?

Ch. 4

Explores knowledge as force for social change – using examples of knowledge society, consumer society and risk society, explores different forms of uncertainty and question of how democratic and advantageous 'knowledge explosion' might be.

EVIDENCE AND EXAMPLES

Ch. 1

SIDS – contrasts soc. sci. and nat. sci. historical evidence.

Ch. 2

Quantitative data on church attendance and beliefs.

Qualitative data on new spirituality and meaning of religion.

Ch. 3

Key debates over economic, political, cultural challenges provide testing ground for strength and plausibility of political ideologies.

Ch. 4

Links material from Chs 1, 2 and 3.

Shift from production to consumption.

Empirical examples of social and economic change and responses of social sciences.

AUDIO AND TV

TV 05 on parenting – sleep and MMR problems for parents. Note examples of diverse sources of expert information. Complexity of reading and using that information amongst public.

Now, the last of our linking exercises. Look back over your notes on Block 5 and think about the connections between this material and that in Section 2 on the city.

ACTIVITY 11

How can we link this material to our discussion of cities? In order to practise applying course material to a specific issue we would like you to think about how the material on knowledge and the social sciences, and especially knowledge and social change, applies to contemporary cities.

COMMENT

We came up with this summary on the city and knowledge:

- Cities, in diverse ways, have been transformed by information technology, new knowledge networks and industries, combining with processes of globalization, as well as social polarization.

- People who have access to knowledge, especially the new knowledges, also have access to power.

- Cities have been shaped by a struggle between different ways of knowing and imagining cities.

- Cities are linked by global knowledge networks.

- The contemporary diversity of people in cities, especially those who are able to exercise more agency and power in shaping the design of cities, has yet to produce a consensus on cities or find ways of effectively regulating inequalities in power and cities.

4 THE COURSE THEMES

In DD100 the course themes provide frameworks for linking material across the course and for accessing the big debates with which we engage. In this section we are going to use the three course themes to illustrate how each theme can be used to inform the selection of material across the course.

4.1 Uncertainty and diversity

One of the main functions of the course theme of uncertainty and diversity has been to allow you to explore the extent of economic, social, political and cultural change in the UK in the latter half of the twentieth century and to encourage you, as a social scientist, to think historically. Above all, it has provided a means of raising important questions about this period. We have drawn up a summary of its use in DD100; this is reproduced as Table 1.

TABLE 1   Uncertainty and diversity

Course material	Uncertainty	Diversity
Introductory Chapter	Fear of crime and sense of insecurity on the rise?	Moral panics as response to threats of deviant diversity.
Book 1, Chapter 1	Traditional gender, class, ethnic identities under challenge as social structures change. Re-evaluation of age/body as source of identity – norms of youth able-bodiedness challenged.	Collective action leads to creation and entrenchment of new cultural identities.
Book 1, Chapter 2	New patterns of gender identity, uncertainty for boys?	Fuzzy categories, new opportunities for girls?
Book 1, Chapter 3	Increasing complexity of economic structures makes old class identities less plausible.	Consumption-based identities suggest greater diversity of identities possible.
Book 1, Chapter 4	Impact of racialization and ethnicization. Britishness and Englishness more uncertain identities.	Promise of multi-ethnic diversity but persistent blockage of racism, individual and institutional.
TV 01: *Defining Moments*	What does it mean to be British in the 1990s? What rituals are appropriate for national occasions?	Diana's funeral appears to encompass and represent a much more diverse nation than the establishment at Churchill's funeral.

Course material	Uncertainty	Diversity
Book 2, Chapter 1	Can there be any certainty about human nature? Attempts to secure definitions historically and in different disciplines.	What constitutes human nature changes over time. Historical shifts. Interrelationship between social, psychological and biological aspects.
Book 2, Chapter 2	Dominance of medical model and expert medical knowledge challenged and undermined.	Medical model challenged by diverse health belief systems.
Book 2, Chapter 4	Environmental dangers with unpredictable consequences appear to be on the rise. Expert scientific and political knowledge challenged.	Challenges of environmentalism to present new ideas.
TV 02: *The Unusual Suspects*		Changing attitudes and definitions of disability lead to huge diversity of lives for people with disabilities.
Book 3, Chapter 2	Position of men in families and male identities more uncertain.	Family forms increasingly complex and diverse.
Book 3, Chapter 3	Increasingly flexible work makes working lives more uncertain.	Workforce increasingly gender diverse. Forms of work more complex.
Book 3, Chapter 4	Security delivered by post-war welfare state brought into question.	Welfare state forced to confront and respond to more diverse families, lifestyles, working lives. Impact of New Labour.
TV 03: *Living with Risk*	Evidence of insecurity and complexity in the labour market.	
Book 4, Chapter 2		Does cultural globalization create a more unified, homogenous global culture, or create a diversity of new hybrid cultures?
Book 4, Chapter 3	Does economic globalization produce greater uncertainty and instability in the world economic system? Does it make the power and autonomy of nation-states more uncertain?	
Book 4, Chapter 4	Has the decline of the old Westphalian order produced a more unruly, unregulatable global political system? Are new forms of geo-governance a potential source of stability and certainty?	
TV 04: *Global Fantasy II*		Games culture and the Japanese experience of both unifying and hybridized cultural flows.

Course material	Uncertainty	Diversity
Book 5, Chapter 1	Legitimacy and authority of medicine and science, challenged and undermined.	New sources of knowledge.
Book 5, Chapter 2	Decline of trust in religious knowledge and dominant moral codes.	Emergence of a greater range of spiritual frameworks and belief systems in post-war UK.
Book 5, Chapter 3	Decline of trust in political elites, uncertainty around dominant political ideologies and capacity to cope with new issues such as the environment.	Challenge of ecological and feminist movements.
Book 5, Chapter 4	Breakdown of certainty of overarching theories. Advocates of a risk society argue that safety experts and environmental knowledge all produce uncertainty rather than certainty in current era.	Democratization of knowledge. Knowledge revolution. Resistance to economic domination.
TV 05: *Mother Knows Best?*	Uncertainty around the knowledge of health care professionals of all kinds and government agencies as well, especially MMR case study.	Range of parenting advice and belief systems indicates greater diversity in parenting knowledge and advice.

How can we begin to synthesize all of this material together? To some extent, many of these debates about uncertainty and diversity are linked to a common narrative. At the core of this interlocking narrative is the contrast between the contemporary experience of uncertainty and diversity and an earlier era of certainty and uniformity: what is often depicted as a 'golden age'. In both eras the two terms reinforce each other. A uniform society was simpler, offering fewer choices and therefore it underwrote certainties about who we were, what we could do and expect, etc. Similarly, with the emergence of a more diverse society the answers to the same questions became more complex and more uncertain.

As the summary in Table 1 shows, it wasn't merely uniformity that delivered certainty in these narratives. The post-Second World War years were often depicted as an era of social stability of secure, functioning institutions and established reliable patterns of behaviour. Low crime, full employment, a benign welfare state, and trusted systems of expert knowledge: scientists, doctors and politicians. These have been counterposed to an era of unstable, dysfunctional institutions, unreliable and anti-social behaviour, and a collapse in trust in expert knowledge systems and their simple dichotomies. What has linked these two eras have been fundamental patterns of *social change*.

4.2 Structure and agency

Now to the second DD100 theme, structure and agency. By now you'll be aware that the relationship between structure and agency is a key issue in the social sciences. Broadly speaking the debate is about agents – who can be individuals or collectivities – and how they both are constrained by structures and, at the same time, reproduce structures. The debate reflects on the autonomy which we enjoy as individuals or collectivities to think and act as we choose, the constraints and the external pressures which limit this freedom, and about how structures are reproduced through social action.

By now you've done a great deal of work on structure and agency. The Introductory Block introduced you to four different explanations of crime which focused either on individual agency or structural approaches (which look to broader social structures to explain crime). You encountered three different sorts of structure: the biological, the economic and the cultural.

In Block 1 you examined the processes involved in identity formation which are both individual and collective. On the one hand, it was clear that identities can be chosen and must be actively taken up by agents, but on the other hand the repertoire of roles and identities and possibilities that are available to us are clearly structured, in biological, geographical, economic, cultural and political terms.

Block 2 began with an examination of various explanations of human nature and the interrelationship between social, biological and psychological factors. Chapter 3 of Book 2 examined markets in terms of opportunities (for individual choice) and the constraints (of structures) which operate on this freedom. Moreover, the chapter argued that through the amalgamation of individual decisions and deductions broader structures (such as the market) are reproduced.

Block 3 enriched our account of structure and agency by introducing the concepts of power, order and institutions into the debate. Let's pause for a moment to look at Block 3's account of power and its relationship to structure and agency.

Block 3 develops two broad theories of power drawing on the work of Weber and Foucault. Both theories acknowledge different modes of power – domination, authority and persuasion – which draw on different kinds of structure and resources, but the theories deal with them differently, allot them different levels of importance and, as a consequence, deal with structure and agency differently. Drawing some of these theories together we came up with Table 2, which is an amalgamation of our comments on Workbook Activities 1.5 and 1.6 in *Workbook 3*, p.69.

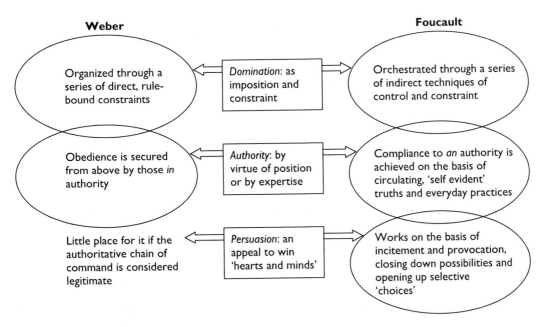

FIGURE 12   Two theories of power

TABLE 2   Power, structure and agency

	Agency	Structure
Weber	Agents excise power. Agents' power comes from their positions in organizations.	Structures determine the powers of agents. Structure disperses power and gives top-down control. Individuals as agents are heavily constrained by structures.
Foucault	Power works on and through agents. Anonymous forces (ideas, expectations) work on agents. By working with these forces agents themselves are part of the exercise of power.	Structures constrain people by closing down other possibilities. Structures are produced through the negotiation of power. Complex and changing networks as much as fixed structures shape power.

In Block 4 we saw that all structures, be they specific institutions or the patterns of social stratification such as the distribution of wealth, are spatially organized. Some structures are local, some national, some regional, and some global. Interestingly, as the focus of DD100 moved from the UK to the global arena, some of the things we had described earlier as structures (the national market, an individual corporation or a nation-state) are also now seen as agents; nation-states, for example, can be thought of as actors in the international system, and firms become agents in competitive global markets. So what is a structure and what is an agent is not always entirely clear. It depends on what it is that we are seeking to understand and what spatial level we are focusing on.

Finally, in Block 5, we examined how knowledge is a structure which shapes agency. Chapter 3 looked at political ideologies, and here you saw clearly how a body of knowledge shapes beliefs at the popular level, but is also used as a tool by politicians and political, social movements to achieve political change.

We have summarized these arguments in Table 3.

TABLE 3   Structure and agency

Course material	Structure	Agency
Book 1, Chapter 1	Class, gender, ethnicity, and body all influence identity formation.	Individual projects, and collectively, class, ethnicity, resistance to racism are examples of agency.
Book 1, Chapter 2	Gender, social, cultural structures shape identities and their development through educational experience.	Group action – educational policies, individual agency, child rearing practices.
Book 1, Chapter 3	Class, poverty, inequality are structures which constrain people and limit their autonomy.	Collective action, e.g. class action, trade union action can influence and re-form structures. Groups and individuals can resist constraining structures.
Book 1, Chapter 4	'Race', 'ethnicity', state, racialized, ethnicized structures influence and constrain identity formation.	Collective action to re-form ethnicized identities resistance to racism.
Book 2, Chapter 1	Social, biological, psychological structures are all involved in natural/social interaction.	Individual agency influences structures.
Book 2, Chapter 2	Social, state structures inform health care.	Collective action, complementary medicine, challenges traditional authodoxy.
Book 2, Chapter 3	Economic markets, capitalist economy, 'externalities', 'invisible hand' of the market.	Collective and individual action, e.g. consumers.
Book 2, Chapter 4	'Outer nature', environment, state, government policies illustrate influences in natural/social relationship.	Collective agency, action to resist environmental crises, awareness of risk.
Book 3, Chapter 1	Sources of power – hierarchies, diffuse operation of power, indirect/direct power, institutional corporate power, state power.	Collective action, resistance to economic power.
Book 3, Chapter 2	Patriarchy, gender structures, family as an institution.	Feminist challenges and women's resistance to male power, new, diverse family forms, changes for women and men.
Book 3, Chapter 3	Economic institutions, work – paid, domestic, gendered structures of work.	Re-formation of work through individual and collective action.
Book 3, Chapter 4	Welfare institutions, state policy, class, gender, ethnicity differences.	Political ideologies, new political movements, challenges to orthodoxy.

Course material	Structure	Agency
Book 4, Chapter 1	Globalization as a set of processes. Western powers especially USA. Cultural economic, political globalization.	Resistance to globalization – historically and by local societies.
Book 4, Chapter 2	Cultural globalization, Western, US culture, media industries.	Local societies retain their cultures and make their own use of global media cultures.
Book 4, Chapter 3	Economic globalization, economic inequalities.	Traditional economic relations, local resistance.
Book 4, Chapter 4	Political globalization, dominant political systems.	Local resistance to global political dominance.
Book 5, Chapter 1	Medical, scientific, patriarchal institutions, orthodox medicine, 'expert' knowledge.	Collective action, complementary medicine, feminist challenges.
Book 5, Chapter 2	Religious orthodoxy, established religions, traditional religions, hierarchies of religious knowledge.	New spirituality, feminist challenges, New Age diversity.
Book 5, Chapter 3	'Outer nature', environmental degradation, traditional political ideologies as source of expertise.	Ecologism, feminist challenges, new ecology movements.
Book 5, Chapter 4	Knowledge explosion, access to 'expert' knowledge, 'risk society' constrains agency.	Widespread dissemination of and access to knowledge makes for greater democracy, 'knowledge society' and 'consumer society' create opportunities.

4.3 Knowledge and knowing

The third DD100 course theme is that of knowledge and knowing which looks at both the changing nature of what counts as knowledge and the importance of knowledge systems and at the processes that are involved in the production of knowledge. For social scientists this includes the methods that we use in seeking evidence to support the claims and theories that we offer to explain social phenomena. The knowledge and knowing theme includes the narrative description of changes in knowledge over time and the ways in which knowledge provides explanations for change and the operation of social relations. We have illustrated this through the course using the circuit of knowledge.

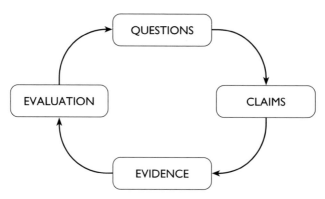

FIGURE 13   The circuit of knowledge

We have drawn up a summary of the knowledge and knowing theme in Table 4.

TABLE 4   Knowledge and knowing

Course material	Knowledge and knowing
Introductory Block	Introduction to the circuit of knowledge in *Introductory Chapter* and *Workbook*. Questions and claims. Quantative evidence. Different explanantions of crime.
Book 1, Chapter 1	Questions about identity: How is it formed? How much control do we have? Is there more uncertainty about identity now?
Book 1, Chapter 2	What evidence is there about gender identities? Evidence of educational achievement. Evidence of change over time.
Book 1, Chapter 3	Claims about class and identity. Theories of Marx and Weber.
Book 1, Chapter 4	Claims about processes of racialization and ethnicization evidence of change – official statistics, critique of texts.
Workbook 1	Structure of an argument.
TV 01: *Defining Moments*	Knowledge of change. Different knowledge about changing British identities.
Study Skills Supplement 1: Reading Visual Images	Visual images as evidence.
Book 2, Chapter 1	Claims about human nature – social, biological, psychological explanations. Changing knowledge over time.
Book 2, Chapter 2	Explanations of different knowledge about health. Models changing knowledge over time.
Book 2, Chapter 3	Economic models. Quantitative evidence.
Book 2, Chapter 4	Explanations of relationship between natural and social. Changing story of this relationship, growth of 'risk society'.

Study Skills Supplement 2: Reading Evidence	Qualitative and quantitative evidence.
TV 02: *The Unusual Suspects*	Changing knowledge about disability.
Book 3, Chapter 1	Different theories of power.
Book 3, Chapter 2	Claims about operation of power in families. Explanations and evidence. Change in families over time. New knowledge.
Book 3, Chapter 3	Quantitative evidence. Models. Knowledge of change over time.
Book 3, Chapter 4	Different political ideologies – explanations and programmes for action. Changing knowledge in post-war UK.
TV 03: *Living with Risk*	Narrative of change in context of employment and work.
Workbook 3	Comparison of different theories.
Book 4	Concepts and theories.
Book 4, Chapter 1	Competing theories.
Book 4, Chapter 2	Argument about cultural globalization.
Book 4, Chapter 3	Inter-nationalist theories of economic globalization. Quantitative evidence.
Book 4, Chapter 4	Transformationalist theory of political globalization.
TV 04: *Global Fantasy II*	Narrative of change. Different explanations of growth of computer games globally.
Study Skills Supplement 3: Reading Maps	Maps as evidence.
Workbook 4	Evaluation of theories' strengths and weaknesses.
Book 5, Chapter 1	Narrative of changing knowledge about medical science. What is knowledge? – ideas, practices, ways of thinking about and understanding the world which guide action and thought. Natural sciences and social sciences.
Book 5, Chapter 2	Narrative of changes in religious knowledge. Evidence to support claims. How do social scientists know? Positivist, interpretavist methods.
Book 5, Chapter 3	What do we do about the knowledge we have? How can knowledge inform action? Political ideologies. Challenges to traditional ideologies and new knowledge about the environment.
Book 5, Chapter 4	Knowledge and the social sciences – narrative of change in knowledge society, move from production to consumption, risk society, social science knowledge about these changes. Is there greater democracy with advent of 'knowledge society'?
TV 05: *Mother Knows Best?*	Changing knowledge, a new 'knowledge society'? Sources of expertise, challenge to traditional experts, e.g. about child care and MMR.
Workbook 5	Circuit of knowledge. Comparison of different kinds of knowledge.

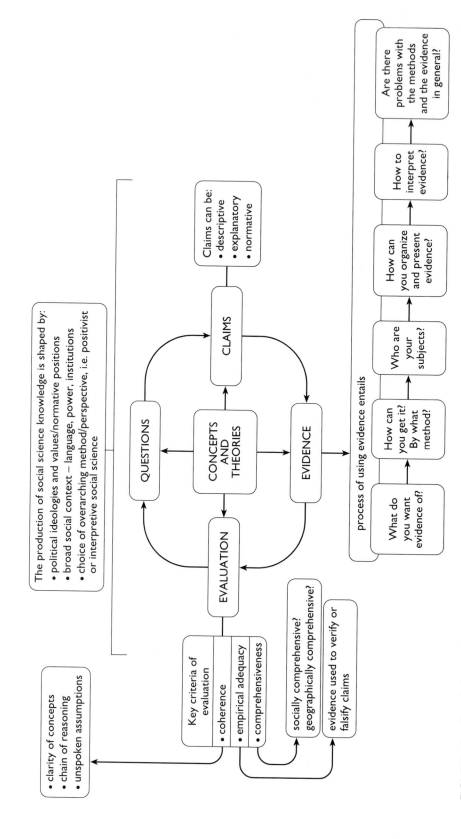

FIGURE 14   Knowledge and knowing: Introductory Block to Block 5 overview

It will also be useful for your work towards TMA 06 and in any future study you undertake in the social sciences to think about the kind of questions you need to ask when you are weighing up particular kinds of knowledge, for example when evaluating theories. What sort of questions do you need to ask when you are assessing the strengths and weaknesses of particular theories or claims made by social scientists?

There are many different ways that you could approach this task and what is shown in Figure 15 is one version for you to think about.

FIGURE 15   Extracting and evaluating the epistemological basis of social science arguments

(1)   What are the key questions being asked?

(2)   What are the key claims being made?

(3)   Is it possible to separate out descriptive, explanatory, and normative claims? Pause before moving on to evidence. Try and consider something of the social context of the argument and its theoretical origins.

(4)   Think carefully about the key concepts that the text appears to use. Do they cluster together? Do they appear to be implicitly or explicitly arranged in a theoretical framework? Ask yourself whether these concepts and theories have asked the most open set of questions. Have they also closed down options and created absences that should be investigated?

(5)   If it is not explicitly stated, can you work back from concepts, theory and the character of claims (especially any normative claims) to the wider social science context from which the arguments have sprung? Can you deduce the presence of any particular set of values, political ideologies, specific institutional origins, or overriding social science method/model: positivist or interpretive?

(6)   What evidence has been amassed to support and shape the argument? To which specific claims and questions does the evidence speak?

(7)   How was that evidence obtained, by whom, by what methods, and about what subject population?

(8)   How has the evidence been presented, organized and interpreted? How have the initial concepts and theories shaped the selection and interpretation of evidence?

(9)   Has the argument been evaluated? Has it been compared with any other arguments? What does the text itself claim?

(10)   Can you apply the key tests of coherence, empirical adequacy and comprehensiveness to weigh up the strengths and weaknesses of the argument(s)?

(11)   What new questions came out of the process of evaluation? How do the original claims fare, when examined?

(12)   Overall, how have the broad social context and political values of the work shaped its internal detail?

5 TMA 06

In order to start your work on TMA 06 you will need to gather the notes from your earlier work on DD100. However, the first thing you need to do is to decide which question you are going to answer. In TMA 06 for the first time on DD100 you have a choice. This means looking at the questions and unpacking them in terms of the task you are being asked to undertake. It would be useful to look first at the 'process' words that are involved. Audio-cassette 10, Side A gives more advice on approaching TMA 06.

Each of the choices for TMA 06 always requires you to draw on at least three blocks of the course so your selection of material will be the next step once you have decided on your question. This means that you can choose material from the Introductory Block, Blocks 1, 2, 3, 4 or 5.

- You will need to make some brief notes, rather as we have here, outlining the sorts of material that will be relevant. Start with the key questions, themes and debates before you check the sources of material in different blocks in the course.

- The next stage is to select appropriate material from across the different blocks of DD100 (checking that you have included material from at least three).

- You will need to make a plan, based on how you are going to approach the question and the strategies that you are going to adopt in order to answer the question set.

- Synthesis and integration means starting with the question and using examples. Fit your notes to the TMA and not the other way round!

- Use your notes to trace the threads between blocks. Claims and evidence should come first, so that you use your notes to support what you are writing in your essay rather than just summarizing the different blocks.

- Link the ideas in different parts of the course, for example as we have done in this block in exploring social change and the city.

Good luck!

 You should now turn to the *Assignments Booklet* for TMA 06.

REFERENCES

Boal, F.W. (1995) *Shaping a City: Belfast in the Late Twentieth Century*, Belfast, The Institute of Irish Studies, The Queen's University of Belfast.

Daunton, M.J. (1977) *Coal Metropolis, Cardiff, 1870–1914*, London, Leicester University Press.

Engels, F. (1987, first published 1845) *The Conditions of the Working Class in England*, Harmondsworth, Penguin.

Jordan, G. and Weedon, C. (1995) *Cultural Politics: Class, Gender, Race and the Postmodern World*, Oxford, Blackwell.

Parker, T. (1994) *May the Lord in His Mercy be Kind to Belfast*, London, HarperCollins.

Social Trends, London, The Stationery Office for Office for National Statistics (annual).

ACKNOWLEDGEMENTS

Grateful acknowledgement is made to the following sources for permission to reproduce material in this review.

Figures

Figure 3: © Paul Mattsson/Reportdigital.co.uk; Figure 4: © The National Gallery London; Figure 5: Boal, F.W. (1995) *Shaping a City: Belfast in the Late Twentieth Century*, The Institute of Irish Studies, The Queen's University of Belfast/The Northern Ireland Housing Executive. © F.W. Boal and The Northern Ireland Housing Executive; Figure 6: magazine advert for Cardiff Bay, 2 May 1992. By permission of Cardiff Bay Development Corporation; Figures 7 and 8: Mike Levers/The Open University; Figure 9: © Paul Box/ Reportdigital.co.uk; Figure 10: © Frank Monaco/Rex Features; Figure 11: © Dennis Stone/Rex Features.

Cover

Images copyright © 1996 PhotoDisc, Inc.

STUDY SKILLS INDEX

IWB = *Introductory Workbook*
WB1 = *Workbook 1*
WB2 = *Workbook 2*
WB3 = *Workbook 3*
WB4 = *Workbook 4*
AC7A = *Notes for Audio-cassette 7, Side A*
WB5 = *Workbook 5*
ECR = *End of Course Review*
AC10A = Audio-cassette 10, Side A